*In the name of Allah
The Merciful, the Compassionate*

Presented to ....

....

From ....

Date ....

Other Goodword books on Islam

- Tell Me About the Prophet Muhammad
- Tell Me About the Prophet Musa
- Tell Me About the Prophet Yusuf
- Tell Me About Hajj
- A Handbook of Muslim Belief
- The Moriscos of Spain
- The Story of Islamic Spain
- Spanish Islam
- A Simple Guide to Islam's Contribution to Science
- The Quran, Bible and Science
- Islamic Medicine
- Islam and the Divine Comedy
- Decisive Moments in the History of Islam
- My Discovery of Islam
- Islam At the Crossroads
- The Spread of Islam in the World
- The Spread of Islam in France
- The Islamic Art and Architecture
- The Islamic Art of Persia
- The Hadith for Beginners
- Islamic Thought and its Place in History
- Muhammad: The Hero As Prophet
- A History of Arabian Music
- A History of Arabic Literature
- Ever Thought About the Truth?
- Crude Understanding of Disbelief
- The Miracle in the Ant
- Allah is Known Through Reason
- The Basic Concepts in the Quran
- The Moral Values of the Quran
- The Beautiful Commands of Allah
- The Beautiful Promises of Allah
- The Muslim Prayer Encyclopaedia
- After Death, Life!
- Living Islam: Treading the Path of Ideal
- A Basic Dictionary of Islam
- The Muslim Marriage Guide
- A Treasury of the Quran
- The Quran for All Humanity
- The Quran: An Abiding Wonder
- The Call of the Qur'an
- Muhammad: A Prophet for All Humanity
- Words of the Prophet Muhammad
- An Islamic Treasury of Virtues
- Islam and Peace
- Introducing Islam
- The Moral Vision
- Principles of Islam
- God Arises
- Islam: The Voice of Human Nature
- Islam: Creator of the Modern Age
- Woman Between Islam and Western Society
- Woman in Islamic Shari'ah
- Islam As It Is
- Religion and Science
- Tabligh Movement
- The Soul of the Quran
- Presenting the Quran
- The Wonderful Universe of Allah
- Selections from the Noble Reading
- Heart of the Koran
- Muhammad: A Mercy to all the Nations
- The Sayings of Muhammad
- The Life of the Prophet Muhammad
- History of the Prophet Muhammad
- A-Z Steps to Leadership

Polygamy
and Islam

Maulana Wahiduddin Khan

Goodword
B·O·O·K·S

Translated by Farida Khanam

Urdu version: *Taadud-e-Azwaj*
Hindi version: *Bahu Patniwad aur Islam*

First published 1984
© Goodword Books, 2004
Reprinted 1992, 1995, 1996, 1998, 1999, 2001, 2004

NO COPYRIGHT
This book does not carry a copyright.
Goodword Books, New Delhi being a non-profit making institution, gives its permission to reproduce this book in any form or to translate it into any language for the propagation of the Islamic cause.

Heavy discount is available on bulk purchase of this book for distribution purpose.

GOODWORD BOOKS PVT. LTD.
1, Nizamuddin West Market
New Delhi- 110 013
e-mail: info@goodwordbooks.com
www.goodwordbooks.com

Printed in India

Contents

Polygamy and Islam 7

The Inequality in Numbers 10

The Willingness of Women 13

The Solution to a Problem rather than a Commandment 16

Unlawful Polygamy 18

The Islamic Way 19

Conclusion 21

Notes 23

بسم الله الرحمن الرحيم

Polygamy and Islam

In terms of the birth rate, men and women are almost equal in number. But subsequently, for a variety of reasons, the number of men in society decreases, leaving an excess of women. Now the question arises as to what should be the solution to this problem. In view of the inevitability of this imbalance, how is a healthy relationship between the sexes to be established? The choice for us, therefore, is not between monogamy and polygamy, but rather, between the lawful polygamy of Islam or the illicit polygamy of non-Islamic peoples.

One of the commandments given in the Qur'an as a matter of social organization concerns polygamy, that is permission for a man to marry up to four women:

> *If you fear that you cannot treat orphans with fairness, then you may marry such women (widowed) as seem good to you: two, three or four of them. But if you fear that you cannot do justice, marry one only.*[1]

This verse was revealed after the Battle of Uhud (Shawwal 3 A.H.) in which seventy Muslims were martyred. Suddenly, seventy homes in Medina were bereft of all male members, and the question arose as to how all these widows and orphans were to be cared for. This was an acute social problem. It was solved by the revelation of this verse asking the people who could afford it to take care of the orphans, by marrying the widows and keeping their orphaned children under their guardianship.

The background and wording of this verse appear to express a commandment which should be only temporary in effect. That is to say that it applied only to a particular state of emergency when, due to loss of men in battle, the number of women exceeded the number of available men. But the Qur'an, despite its having been revealed at a particular time and place, is universal in its application. One of the great characteristics of the Qur'an is that it describes eternal realities, with reference to temporal issues, this commandment being typical of this special quality of the Qur'an.

One point greatly in need of clarification is the fact that in the matter of marrying more than one woman, the initiative does not lie solely with any individual man. There is always the condition—an inescapable one—that whatever the society, the women should outnumber the men. Suppose the earth were inhabited by one billion people out of which 500 million were men and 500 million were women. It would not then be possible in such a situation for a man to have more than one wife. A second, third or fourth wife would be obtained only by force. But in Islam, a forced marriage is not considered lawful. According to the *shari'ah* the willingness of the bride-to-be is a compulsory condition.

Looked at from a practical angle, the above commandment of the Qur'an can be complied with only if that particular situation exists in society which existed in Medina after the Battle of Uhud—that is, there is a disproportion in the ratio of men and women. In the absence of such a situation, this commandment of the Qur'an would be inapplicable. But studies of human society and its history have shown that the situation in ancient Medina was not one which existed only at a particular point in time. It is a situation which had almost always been prevalent throughout the entire world. That situation of emergency is, in fact, the general situation of mankind. This commandment is yet another proof of God's omniscience. His commandment, seemingly elicited by an emergency, became an eternal commandment for the whole of our world.

The Inequality in Numbers

Records show that male and female births are almost equal in number. But a study of mortality shows that the rate is higher for men than for women. This disparity is in evidence from early childhood to extreme old age. According to the Encyclopaedia Britannica: "In general, the risk of death at any given age is less for females than for males."[2]

The proportionately higher numbers of women in society can be traced to a variety of causes. For instance, when war breaks out, the majority of the casualties are men. In the First World War (1914-18) about 8 million soldiers were killed. Most of the civilians killed were also men. In the Second World War (1939-45) about 60 million people were either killed or maimed for life, most of them men. In the Iraq-Iran war alone (1979-1988), 82,000 Iranian women and about 100,000 Iraqi women were widowed. All in the space of ten years.

Another drain on the availability of men in society is imprisonment. In the U.S., the most civilized society of modern times, no less than 1,300,000 people are convicted daily for one crime or another. A number of them—97% of whom are men—are obliged to serve lengthy prison sentences.[3]

The modern industrial system too is responsible for the lower proportion of men in society, death by accident having become a matter of daily routine in present times. There is no country in which accidents do not take place every day on the streets, in the factories and wherever sophisticated, heavy machinery is handled by human beings. In this modern industrial age, such accidents are so much on the increase that a whole new discipline has come into being—safety engineering. According to data collected in 1967, in that year a total of 175,000 people died as the result of accidents in fifty different countries. Most of these were men.[4]

In spite of safety engineering, casualties from industrial accidents have increased. For instance, the number of air accidents in 1988 was higher than ever before. Similarly, experimentation in arsenals continues to kill people in all industrialized countries, but the death toll is never made public.

Here again, it is men who have the highest casualty rate.

For reasons of this nature, women continue to outnumber men. This difference persists in even the most developed societies, e.g. in America. According to data collected in 1967, there were nearly 7,100,000 more women than men. This means that even if every single man in America got married, 7,100,000 women would be left without husbands.

We give below the data of several western countries to show the ratio of men to women.[6]

Country	Male	Female
Austria	47.7%	52.93%
Burma	48.81	51.19
Germany	48.02	51.89
France	48.99	51.01
Italy	48.89	51.01
Poland	48.61	51.30
Spain	48.94	51.06
Switzerland	48.67	51.33
Soviet Union	46.59	53.03
United States	48.58	51.42

The Willingness of Women

The presence of a greater number of women in a society is not the only prerequisite for polygamy. It is, in addition, compulsory that the woman who is the object of the man's choice should be willing to enter into the married state. This willingness on the woman's part is a must before a marriage can be lawful in Islam. It is unlawful to marry a woman by force. There is no example in the history of Islam where a man has been allowed to force a woman into marriage.

The Prophet Muhammad's own view that "an unmarried girl should not be married until her permission has been taken"[6] had been recorded by both Bukhari and Muslim. 'Abdullah ibn 'Abbas, one of the Prophet's Companions and a commentator on the Qur'an, narrates the story of a girl who came to the Prophet complaining that her father had her married off against her wishes. The Prophet gave her the choice of either remaining within the bonds of wedlock or of freeing herself from them.[7]

Another such incident narrated by 'Abdullah ibn 'Abbas concerns a woman called Burairah and her husband, Mughith, who was a black slave. 'Abdullah ibn 'Abbas tells the story as if it were all happening before his very eyes: "Mughith is following Burairah through the paths of Medina. He is crying and his tears are running down his beard. Seeing him, the Prophet said to me, 'O 'Abbas, are you not surprised at Mughith's love for Burairah and Burairah's hate for Mughith?' Then the Prophet said to Burairah, 'I wish you would take him back.' Burairah said to the Prophet, 'Is that a command?' The Prophet replied, 'No, it is only a recommendation.' Then Burairah said, 'I don't need your recommendation.'"[8]

There was an interesting case of polygamy which took place during the Caliphate of 'Umar ibn al-Khattab. A certain widow, Umm Aban bint 'Utbah had four suitors for marriage. All four—'Umar ibn al-Khattab, 'Ali ibn abi Talib, Zubayr and Talhah—were already married. Umm Aban accepted the proposal of marriage made by Talhah and, of course, refused the other three, whereupon she was married to Talhah.[9]

This happened in Medina, the capital of the

Islamic State. Among the rejected suitors was the reigning Caliph. But no one expressed even surprise or dismay, the reason being that in Islam, a woman is completely free to make her own decisions. This is a right that no one can take away from her—not even the ruler of the day.

These incidents show that the Islamic commandments giving permission to marry up to four women does not mean having the right to seize four women and shut them up inside one's home. Marriage is a matter of mutual consent. Only that woman can be made a second or a third wife who is willing to be so. And when this matter rests wholly on the willingness of the woman, there is no cause for objection.

The present age gives great importance to freedom of choice. This value is fully supported by Islamic law. On the other hand, the upholders of "feminism" want to turn freedom of choice into restriction of choice.

The Solution to a Problem rather than a Commandment

The above discussion makes it clear that the difference in number of men and women is a permanent problem existing in both war and peace. Now the question arises as to how to solve this problem. What should those women do to satisfy their natural urges when they have failed to find a husband in a monogamous society? And how are they to secure an honorable life in that society?

One way — hallowed in Indian tradition — is for widows to burn themselves to death, so that neither they nor their problems survive. The alternative is to allow themselves to be turned out of their homes on to the streets. The state of Hindu society resulting from adherence to this principle can be judged from a detailed report published in *India Today*[10] entitled "Widows: Wrecks of Humanity."

Now there is no need to discuss this further, because it is inconceivable that in present times any sensible person would advocate this as a solution.

The other possible 'solution' to be found in the 'civilized' society of the West is the conversion of unwillingness to become a second wife into willingness to become a mistress, often of more than one man.

During the Second World War, in which several western countries such as Germany, France, Britain, etc. took part, a large number of men were killed. As a result, women far outnumbered men at the end of the hostilities. Permissiveness then became the order of the day, to the extent that boards with such inscriptions as "Wanted: A Guest for the Evening" could be seen outside the homes of husbandless women. This state of affairs persisted in western countries in various forms, even long after the war, and is now largely prevalent because of industrial and mechanical accidents.

Unlawful Polygamy

People who would outlaw polygamy have to pay the price. That is, they are forced to tolerate men and women having illicit relations, which is surely a much more unsavory state of affairs. Failure to control a natural process whereby the male population dwindles, leaving "surplus" women, coupled with the outlawing of polygamy, has given rise to the evil of the "mistress" (defined by Webster's Dictionary as "a woman who has sexual intercourse with and, often, is supported by a man for a more or less extended period of time without being married to him; paramour"). This, in effect, sets up a system of illegal polygamy.

The system of keeping a mistress is prevalent in all those countries, including India, where there are legal constraints on polygamy or where polygamy is looked down upon socially. In such a situation, the real problem is not whether or not to adopt polygamy. The real problem is whether or not to legalize its adoption. The problem of surplus women in society can be solved only by polygamy, whether we choose to consider it legal or not.

The Islamic Way

The solution to this problem in the Islamic *shari'ah* is the giving of permission to men, under special conditions, to marry more than one woman. This principle of polygamy, as enshrined in the Islamic *shari'ah* is designed, in actual fact, to save women from the ignoble consequences mentioned above. This commandment, although apparently general in application, was given only as a solution to a specific social problem. It provides an arrangement whereby surplus women may save themselves from sexual anarchy and have a proper stable family life. That is to say, it is not a question of adopting polygamy rather than monogamy. The choice is between polygamy and sexual anarchy.

If the commandment to practice polygamy is seen in the abstract, it would appear to be biased in favor of men. But when placed in the context of social organization, it is actually in favor of women. Polygamy is both a proper and a natural solution to women's problems.

The permission to practice polygamy in Islam was not given in order to enable men to satisfy their sexual urges. It was designed as a practical strategy to solve a particular problem. Marrying more than one woman is possible only when there are more women than men. Failing this, it is out of the question. Is it conceivable that Islam, just to satisfy man's desires, would give us a commandment which is neither possible nor practical?

The *Encyclopaedia Britannica* (1984) aptly concludes that one reason for adopting polygamy is the surplus of women. Among most peoples who permit or prefer it, the large majority of men live in a state of monogamy because of the limited number of women.[160]

To have more than one wife is not an ideal in Islam. It is, in essence, a practical solution to a social problem.

Conclusion

In terms of the birth rate, men and women are almost equal in number. But, subsequently, for a variety of reasons, the number of men in society decreases, leaving an excess of women. Now the question arises as to what should be the solution to this problem. In view of the inevitability of this imbalance, how is a healthy relationship between the sexes to be established?

By following the principle of monogamy, hundreds of thousands of women fail to find husbands for themselves and are thus denied an honorable place in society. Monogamy as an absolute principle may seem pleasing to some, but events show that this is not fully practicable in the world of today. The choice for us, therefore, is not between monogamy and polygamy, but rather between the lawful polygamy of Islam and the illicit polygamy of non-Islamic peoples. The latter system leaves "surplus" women to lead lives of sexual anarchy and social destruction. The former, on the other hand, permits them to opt on their own free will for marriage with anyone who can give fair treatment to more than one wife.

Notes

1. Qur'an, 4:3.
2. *Encyclopaedia Britannica* (1984), vol. 7, p. 37.
3. Ibid, vol 14, p. 1102.
4. Ibid, vol. 16, p. 137.
5. Figures taken from *Encyclopaedia Britannica* (1984).
6. Al-Bukhari, *Sahih, Bab la Yunkihu al-Ab wa Ghairuhu al-Bikra wath-Thayyiba illa bi Ridaha (Fath al-Bari,* 9/157).
7. Abu Dawud, *Sunan,Kitab an-Nikah,* 2/232.
8. Ad-Darimi, *Sunan, Kitab an-Nikah,* 2/170.
9. Ibn Kathir, *Al-Bidayah wa an-Nihayah,* 7/153.
10. *India Today* (New Delhi), November 15, 1987.
11. *Encyclopaedia Britannica* (1984), 8/97.

Goodword English Publications

The Holy Quran: Text, Translation and Commentary (HB), Tr. Abdullah Yusuf Ali

The Holy Quran (PB), Tr. Abdullah Yusuf Ali

The Holy Quran (Laminated Board), Tr. Abdullah Yusuf Ali

The Holy Quran (HB), Tr. Abdullah Yusuf Ali

Holy Quran (Small Size), Tr. Abdullah Yusuf Ali

The Quran, Tr. T.B. Irving

The Koran, Tr. M.H. Shakir

The Glorious Quran, Tr. M.M. Pickthall

Allah is Known Through Reason, Harun Yahya

The Basic Concepts in the Quran, Harun Yahya

Crude Understanding of Disbelief, Harun Yahya

Darwinism Refuted, Harun Yahya

Death Resurrection Hell, Harun Yahya

Devoted to Allah, Harun Yahya

Eternity Has Already Begun, Harun Yahya

Ever Thought About the Truth?, Harun Yahya

The Mercy of Believers, Harun Yahya

The Miracle in the Ant, Harun Yahya

The Miracle in the Immune System, Harun Yahya

The Miracle of Man's Creation, Harun Yahya

The Miracle of Hormones, Harun Yahya

The Miracle in the Spider, Harun Yahya

The Miracle of Creation in DNA, Harun Yahya

The Miracle of Creation in Plants, Harun Yahya

The Moral Values of the Quran, Harun Yahya

The Nightmare of Disbelief, Harun Yahya

Perfected Faith, Harun Yahya